Historical Biographies

KATHERINE JOHNSON
NASA Mathematician

DiscoverRoo
An Imprint of Pop!
popbooksonline.com

by Grace Hansen

WELCOME TO DiscoverRoo!

This book is filled with videos, puzzles, games, and more! Scan the QR codes* while you read, or visit the website below to make this book pop.

https://popbooksonline.com/johnson

abdobooks.com

Published by Pop!, a division of ABDO, PO Box 398166, Minneapolis, Minnesota 55439. Copyright © 2023 by Abdo Consulting Group, Inc. International copyrights reserved in all countries. No part of this book may be reproduced in any form without written permission from the publisher. DiscoverRoo™ is a trademark and logo of Pop!.

Printed in the United States of America, North Mankato, Minnesota.

102022
012023

Cover Photo: Getty Images; Shutterstock Images

Interior Photos: Getty Images; Shutterstock Images; NASA Image Collection; Library of Congress; Dolph Briscoe Center for American History at the University of Texas at Austin

Editor: Elizabeth Andrews

Series Designers: Laura Graphenteen; Neil Klinepier

Library of Congress Control Number: 2022941250

Publisher's Cataloging-in-Publication Data

Names: Hansen, Grace, author.

Title: Katherine Johnson: NASA mathematician / by Grace Hansen

Description: Minneapolis, Minnesota : Pop!, 2023 | Series: Historical biographies | Includes online resources and index.

Identifiers: ISBN 9781098243401 (lib. bdg.) | ISBN 9781098244101 (ebook)

Subjects: LCSH: Johnson, Katherine G.--Juvenile literature. | Women mathematicians--Biography--Juvenile literature. | Afro-American women mathematicians--Biography--Juvenile literature. | Human computers--Biography--Juvenile literature. | United States National Aeronautics and Space Administration--Juvenile literature.

Classification: DDC 510.92 [B]--dc23

*Scanning QR codes requires a web-enabled smart device with a QR code reader app and a camera.

TABLE OF CONTENTS

CHAPTER 1
Thinking in Numbers 4

CHAPTER 2
Overcoming the Odds 6

CHAPTER 3
From Teacher to Computer 12

CHAPTER 4
Out of This World 18

CHAPTER 5
Down to Earth 24

Important Dates 28
Making Connections 30
Glossary 31
Index 32
Online Resources 32

CHAPTER 1

THINKING IN NUMBERS

A young girl living in West Virginia counted her steps as she walked to church. That night after supper, she helped clean the dishes. One by one, she counted the plates and silverware as they were washed and dried. She followed her older brother to school each day. She couldn't wait to start school herself!

WATCH A VIDEO HERE!

Katherine had a love for learning from the start.

The girl's name was Katherine Coleman. She was born in White Sulphur Springs on August 26, 1918. Katherine was gifted from an early age. When she was finally able to attend grade school, she skipped the first grade. Katherine also skipped the fifth grade. At the ripe age of 10, she was on her way to high school.

CHAPTER 2

OVERCOMING THE ODDS

When Katherine was growing up, West Virginia was segregated. This meant that she could not attend school with white children. There was also no high school for Black students in her hometown. Katherine and her siblings had to attend a high school in Institute, West Virginia, 125 miles (201km) from their home.

LEARN MORE HERE!

West Virginia State College students protesting segregation in 1960.

Despite this and being four years younger than her classmates, Katherine thrived. She loved mathematics, especially **geometry**. Her interest in astronomy was sparked when her principal pointed out stars and **constellations** in the sky.

This NASA image shows the Orion Nebula in the constellation of Orion. Orion is one of the most recognized constellations in the night sky.

In 1933, Katherine began attending West Virginia State College on a full scholarship. She took every mathematics course available. She also enjoyed English and French. William Schieffelin Claytor was a professor at the college. He was the third African American to earn a Ph.D. in mathematics. Dr. Claytor became one of Katherine's mentors. He knew Katherine would make a good research mathematician. To prepare Katherine,

DID YOU KNOW? Dr. Claytor created new mathematics classes for Katherine to take while she attended college.

Dr. Claytor taught her an advanced form of geometry.

In 1937, at the age of 18, Katherine completed college with a bachelor's degree in mathematics and French.

Dr. Claytor was born in 1908 in Norfolk, Virginia.

CHAPTER 3
FROM TEACHER TO COMPUTER

After college, Katherine taught in Marion, Virginia. There, she met and married James Francis Goble. Katherine put her education and career on pause when she became pregnant with her first daughter. She and James soon

COMPLETE AN ACTIVITY HERE!

Marion, Virginia, is known for its scenic beauty and rolling hills.

welcomed two more daughters. More than ten years later, Katherine would focus on her passions again.

At a family gathering in 1952, one of Katherine's relatives mentioned an amazing new opportunity. The National Advisory Committee for Aeronautics (NACA) was hiring mathematicians. Katherine and her family moved to Newport News, Virginia, where she could pursue a career with NACA. Later that year, Katherine was hired! In June 1953, her job as a computer began at NACA's West Area Computing Unit.

Johnson poses for a portrait at NASA Langley Research Center in 1960.

Computers were people who did calculations by hand. The work was complex. Computing machines at the time could not handle the amount of calculating that needed to be done at NACA. Katherine and her team of about 20 women processed data and performed calculations for NACA's research engineers.

This 1955 image shows a typical computing area at NACA.

After just two weeks, Katherine was moved to the all-male Flight Research Division. There, she studied data from flight tests and investigated **aeronautic** issues. Around this time, Katherine's husband died of a brain tumor. Remaining focused on her work helped Katherine move forward.

CHAPTER 4

OUT OF THIS WORLD

In October 1957, the Soviet Union launched *Sputnik*, the first artificial satellite. The United States quickly formed the Space Task Group. Katherine and the flight research engineers were part of this group. This time was known as the Space Race. In 1958, NACA became

EXPLORE LINKS HERE!

part of the new National Aeronautics and Space Administration (NASA). Katherine now worked as an airspace technologist. She was tasked with creating the first equations to track flight through space.

Johnson performs calculations with her adding machine nearby.

It was an exciting time for Katherine both personally and at work. She married James A. Johnson in 1959. Meanwhile, she cowrote a special report for NASA that was published in 1960.

On May 5, 1961, NASA sent the first American, Alan Shepard, into space as part of Project Mercury. The **trajectory** of this famous flight was planned by Johnson.

Next, NASA planned for astronaut John Glenn to **orbit** Earth. Johnson's calculations had to account for Earth's gravity, shape, and rotation speed. By this time, NASA

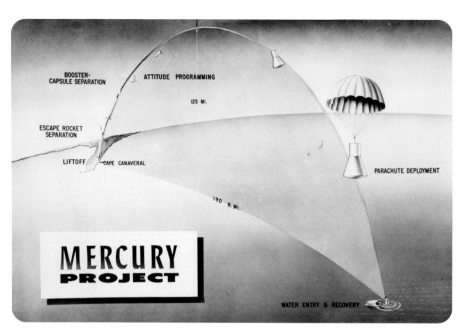

It took a lot of math and careful planning to send Shepard on his 15-minute, 28-second mission.

had electronic computers that did these calculations. But Glenn did not trust them. He wanted Johnson to check the math. She confirmed that the numbers were correct. On February 20, 1962, Glenn safely orbited Earth.

For the next several years, the United States focused its efforts on getting man to the moon. Johnson calculated the flight path for NASA's Apollo 11 mission. She also planned how the Lunar Module *Eagle* would reconnect with space shuttle *Columbia*.

On July 21, 1969, Neil Armstrong and Edwin "Buzz" Aldrin became the first

The Lunar Module Eagle *carrying Armstrong and Aldrin on its ascent to reconnect with* Columbia.

humans to walk on the moon. After 21 hours, the men launched the *Eagle* back into orbit. The *Eagle* now had to reconnect with *Columbia*. Johnson's math was right and the mission was a success! The astronauts safely returned to Earth. Johnson now had six more Apollo missions to plan.

> ### HIDDEN FIGURES
>
> In 2016, Margot Lee Shetterly's book *Hidden Figures* brought attention to NASA's little-known Black, female human computers. In a speech she said, "All eyes [are] on this man as he's going into space and… [Katherine Johnson] stood behind the man and checked the numbers."

CHAPTER 5
DOWN TO EARTH

After 33 successful years with NASA, Johnson retired in 1986. Her accomplishments opened new doors after retirement. She spoke at conferences and schools, inspiring students to pursue careers in STEM.

> "We needed to be assertive as women in those days — assertive and aggressive — and the degree to which we had to be that way depended on where you were. I had to be."

A portrait of Johnson at NASA in 1983.

Johnson has been honored with many awards for putting the United States first in the Space Race. She was

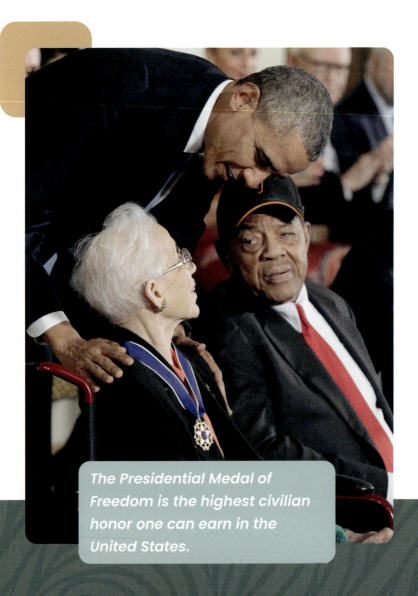

The Presidential Medal of Freedom is the highest civilian honor one can earn in the United States.

awarded the Presidential Medal of Freedom in 2015. In 2016, NASA opened the Katherine G. Johnson Computational Research Facility.

Johnson's work with NASA could be extremely stressful. But it was also incredibly important. And she did it perfectly. Johnson knew that the color of her skin and her gender did not make her any less important in a world where those things seemed to matter. "I don't have a feeling of inferiority. Never had. I'm as good as anybody, but no better."

IMPORTANT DATES

August 26, 1918
Katherine Coleman is born in White Sulphur Springs, West Virginia.

1953
Katherine begins work as a computer at NACA, later NASA.

1929
Katherine begins attending high school at 10 years old.

1960
Johnson is the first female in her division to receive author credit on a research report. In 1961, the report's calculations are put to use sending the first American into space.

FEBRUARY 20, 1962
Astronaut John Glenn safely orbits Earth after he has Johnson check the electronic computer's math for his flight.

NOVEMBER 24, 2015
President Barack Obama presents Katherine Johnson with the Presidential Medal of Freedom.

JULY 24, 1969
Johnson's work brings astronauts Neil Armstrong, Edwin Aldrin, and Michael Collins safely back to Earth after their visit to the moon.

FEBRUARY 24, 2020
Johnson passes away at the age of 101. She is remembered by NASA as "an American hero."

MAKING CONNECTIONS

TEXT-TO-SELF

What do you think was Johnson's greatest accomplishment in her career?

TEXT-TO-TEXT

Have you read any other books about Katherine Johnson and the Black female computers at NASA? What did those books have in common with this one?

TEXT-TO-WORLD

Why do you believe it was important to the United States to get ahead in the Space Race?

GLOSSARY

aeronautic — relating to the science or practice of building or flying aircraft.

artificial satellite — a spacecraft that is sent into orbit around a planet or other space body to gather or send back information.

constellation — a group of stars in the sky that is thought to look like, and is named after, an animal, object, or person.

geometry — the area of mathematics concerned with the study of shapes and objects.

orbit — (noun) the curved path in which a planet, satellite, or spacecraft moves in a circle around another body. (verb) to move in a circle around.

Soviet Union — a country that no longer exists that was made up of fifteen republics in eastern Europe and Northern Asia. Moscow was its capital.

STEM — short for Science, Technology, Engineering, and Math.

trajectory — the actual or expected path of a moving object, especially the curve followed by a spacecraft in flight.

INDEX

Aldrin, Edwin, 22–23
Apollo 11, 22–23
Armstrong, Neil, 22–23
awards and honors, 26–27
birth, 5
Claytor, William Schieffelin, Ph.D., 10–11
computer, 14, 16, 21, 23
education, 5–8, 10
family, 4, 6, 12–14, 17, 20
Glenn, John, 20–21
Goble, James Francis, 12, 17
Johnson, James A., 20
National Advisory Committee for Aeronautics (NACA), 14, 16–18
National Aeronautics and Space Administration (NASA), 19–24
Shepard, Alan, 20
Space Race, 18, 26
teacher, 12
Virginia, 12, 14
West Virginia, 4–7, 10

This book is filled with videos, puzzles, games, and more! Scan the QR codes* while you read, or visit the website below to make this book pop.

https://popbooksonline.com/johnson

*Scanning QR codes requires a web-enabled smart device with a QR code reader app and a camera.